PYTHON

BIBLE

FOR

BEGINNERS

2025

Python programming: Master Coding Fundamentals and Build Real-World Projects with Ease

Richard D. Gault

1

Content

Introduction to Python Bible for Beginners 2025

Python has cemented itself as one of the most versatile and accessible programming languages in the modern tech landscape. Whether you're a novice with no coding experience or someone transitioning from another discipline, Python offers an intuitive gateway into the world of programming. Its simplicity in syntax, coupled with its powerful capabilities, makes it an indispensable tool for professionals and hobbyists alike.

This book, Python Bible for Beginners 2025, is designed to eliminate barriers and provide a structured, hands-on approach to learning Python. In an era where technology evolves rapidly, having foundational knowledge in a language as dynamic as Python is not just an advantage—it's a necessity. Python's relevance spans fields like web development, data science, artificial intelligence, and automation, giving learners practical skills that can be applied across industries.

Why Python?

Python's popularity isn't accidental. It's a language that prioritizes readability and clarity, making it ideal for beginners. Its syntax mirrors natural language, meaning you can focus on problem-solving rather than struggling to decipher complex code structures. Furthermore, Python boasts a vast ecosystem of libraries and frameworks, enabling users to tackle diverse projects with ease.

From automating mundane tasks to analyzing large datasets, Python is a language of endless possibilities. Its growing adoption in educational settings, startups, and large corporations speaks to its versatility and scalability.

Who Is This Book For?

This book is crafted for those who have no prior experience in programming but are eager to explore the potential of Python. Whether you're a student, a professional looking to upskill, or someone exploring coding as a hobby, this guide offers clear, concise instructions to build a solid foundation.

The book also serves as a bridge for individuals who might have some exposure to programming but want to refine their Python knowledge. With carefully designed exercises and practical projects, it allows learners to build confidence in coding through incremental progress.

How This Book Works

The chapters in this book are deliberately structured to take you from the absolute basics to more advanced beginner topics, with each section building on the previous one. By the time you complete the final chapter, you will have created multiple projects and gained an understanding of core Python principles. These projects are designed to reinforce theoretical knowledge and demonstrate how Python solves real-world problems.

In addition to projects, the book emphasizes the importance of coding best practices. Beginners often develop habits that can hinder growth as they advance. Here, you'll learn not just to write code that works, but code that is efficient, readable, and maintainable.

Why Start in 2025?

The landscape of Python development is constantly evolving. As we move into 2025, Python continues to lead with updates that enhance performance, improve developer experience, and expand its range of applications. This book integrates the latest trends and features, ensuring that learners start with the most up-to-date tools and techniques.

For instance, Python 3.12 introduces performance improvements and syntax refinements that reduce boilerplate code. This book incorporates these updates, giving you insights into how Python's latest features can streamline your work.

What You Will Gain

By the end of this journey, you will:

- Have a strong grasp of Python syntax and foundational programming concepts.

- Understand how to solve problems programmatically, breaking complex tasks into manageable steps.

- Be equipped to explore specialized fields like web development, automation, and data analysis.

- Gain the confidence to build your own Python projects, from small tools to more ambitious applications.

Removing the Intimidation Factor

One of the most common barriers to learning programming is fear—fear of complexity, fear of failure, and fear of starting something entirely new. This book addresses these concerns head-on. Concepts are explained in plain language, with real-world analogies where appropriate. Mistakes are treated as learning opportunities rather than setbacks, with plenty of guidance to troubleshoot and debug.

You'll also benefit from a no-nonsense approach. While many programming guides delve into overly technical jargon, Python Bible for Beginners 2025 focuses on clarity and relevance. Each chapter is purposeful, eliminating unnecessary complexity while covering all essential ground.

A Skill for the Future

Python is more than just a coding language; it's a gateway to innovation. It enables learners to build tools that automate tasks, analyze information, and create impactful solutions. As industries increasingly rely on data and software, Python skills can open doors to career opportunities and creative endeavors.

This book is not just about learning Python; it's about discovering how Python can empower you to think logically and solve problems effectively. By developing these skills, you're not just learning a language—you're gaining a new way to approach challenges and opportunities.

Your Journey Starts Here

The chapters ahead will introduce you to concepts step by step, providing examples and exercises designed to reinforce learning. There's no need to rush; the goal is progress, not perfection. With patience and practice, you'll soon find yourself writing Python code with confidence and curiosity.

Whether you aspire to develop applications, automate repetitive tasks, or simply gain a new skill, this book offers everything you need to begin your Python journey in 2025. Let's embark on this exciting adventure together!

Chapter One

Getting Started with Python

Understanding Python and Its Applications

Python is a high-level programming language that prioritizes readability and simplicity. Its versatility has made it one of the most widely used languages globally, with applications in web development, data science, artificial intelligence, and automation. Unlike many programming languages, Python uses an intuitive syntax that resembles natural language, making it particularly beginner-friendly. From automating repetitive tasks to powering complex machine-learning algorithms, Python's scope is vast, allowing users to focus on problem-solving rather than syntax complexities.

Installing Python: Step-by-Step Guide

To begin your Python journey, the first step is to install Python on your computer.

1. Check the Python Version: Ensure your operating system matches the version you select—Windows, macOS, or Linux.

2. Download and Install: Follow the installation prompts, ensuring you check the option to add Python to your system's PATH for command-line accessibility.

3. Verify Installation: Open your terminal or command prompt and type `python --version`. If installed correctly, this command will display the installed Python version.

Setting Up Your Development Environment

Choosing the right tools can streamline your programming experience.

1. Integrated Development Environments (IDEs): Popular IDEs like PyCharm, Visual Studio Code, and Thonny provide features like syntax highlighting, debugging tools, and integrated file management.

2. Text Editors: Lightweight editors such as Sublime Text or Atom can be customized for Python development.

3.Package Management: Tools like pip, which comes bundled with Python, allow you to install and manage Python libraries efficiently.

Writing Your First Python Program

Once your environment is set up, it's time to write your first Python program. Open your IDE or text editor, and type the following code:

```python
print("Welcome to Python!")
```

Save the file with a `.py` extension, and run it through your terminal or IDE. This simple program outputs the message, demonstrating Python's syntax simplicity and clarity.

Python Syntax: The Building Blocks

Python's syntax is designed for clarity and brevity, eliminating the need for unnecessary semicolons or braces. Key components include:

- Indentation: Python relies on indentation to define code blocks, unlike other languages that use curly brackets.
- Comments: Use the `#` symbol for single-line comments to document your code effectively.

- Case Sensitivity: Python differentiates between uppercase and lowercase letters, so `Variable` and `variable` are distinct.

Variables, Data Types, and Comments
Variables in Python are containers for storing data. They are dynamically typed, meaning you don't need to declare their type explicitly. For instance:

name = *"Alice"* # *String type*
age = *25* # *Integer type*
height = *5.6* # *Float type*
is_ student = *True* # *Boolean type* ```
Data types define the kind of value a variable can hold. Common types include integers, floats, strings, booleans, and lists.

Troubleshooting Common Issues
1. Syntax Errors: These occur when Python encounters invalid syntax. Double-check indentation and typos.

2. Module Not Found: Ensure required libraries are installed using pip.

3. Invalid Indentation: Always use consistent spaces or tabs for indentation, as Python enforces strict rules here.

Exercises for Practice

1. Write a program that takes user input and displays a greeting message.

2. Create a script that calculates the area of a rectangle, given its length and width.

3. Experiment with printing different data types and their combinations.

Chapter Two

Python Basics

Introduction to Python Basics

Python Basics provides the foundation required to understand and write Python programs. It focuses on the fundamental elements like syntax, variables, and data types. This chapter aims to ensure a solid grasp of these essentials before progressing to advanced topics.

Writing Your First Python Program

What is a Python Program?
A Python program is a set of instructions written in the Python language to perform specific tasks. These tasks range from

simple arithmetic operations to complex machine-learning models.

Step-by-Step Guide to Writing Your First Program

1. Open a Python Integrated Development Environment (IDE) like IDLE or a text editor such as VS Code.

2. In the editor, type the following:

```python
print("Hello, World!")
```

3. Save the file with a `.py` extension, e.g., `hello_world.py`.

4. Run the program using the IDE or command line by typing:

```bash
python hello_world.py
```

5. The output, "Hello, World!" will appear, signifying the successful execution of your first Python script.

Analyzing the Script
- `print()`: A built-in function that outputs data to the screen.
- `"Hello, World!"`: A string passed to the `print` function to display text.

This simple exercise introduces the syntax and provides an interactive way to see Python in action.

Python Syntax: The Building Blocks

Understanding Python's Simplicity
Python is known for its straightforward and readable syntax, designed to mimic natural language. This reduces learning complexity and promotes productivity.

Key Syntax Features
1. Case Sensitivity: Python differentiates between uppercase and lowercase. For

example, `Variable` and `variable` are distinct identifiers.

2. Indentation: Python uses indentation to define blocks of code instead of braces or brackets. Example:

```python
if True: print("Indentation matters!")
```

3.Comments: Use `#` for single-line comments and triple quotes (`"""` or `"`) for multi-line comments.

```python
# This is a single-line comment
"""This is a
multi-line comment"""
```

Common Errors to Avoid

- Missing colons (`:`) in structures like `if` or `for`.

- Incorrect or inconsistent indentation.

Mastering syntax ensures clean, functional, and maintainable code, a vital skill for every programmer.

Variables, Data Types, and Comments

Introduction to Variables

Variables act as containers for storing data. Unlike many programming languages, Python does not require explicit declaration of variable types.

Declaring Variables

- Syntax: `variable_name = value`
  Example:
  ```python
  name = "Alice"
  age = 25
  is_student = True
  ```

Understanding Data Types

1. Numeric Types: `int`, `float`, `complex`
   Example:

   ```python
   x = 10      # int
   y = 3.14    # float
   z = 1+2j    # complex
   ```

2. String: A sequence of characters enclosed in quotes.
   Example:

   ```python
   message = "Hello, Python!"
   ```

3. Boolean: Represents `True` or `False`.
   Example:

   ```python
   is_active = True
   ```

4. NoneType: Represents null or no value.
   Example:

   ```python
   value = None
   ```

Working with Comments

Comments improve code readability and are essential for documentation purposes. Use comments to explain logic, especially for complex sections.

Best Practices for Variables

- Use descriptive names, e.g., `user_age` instead of `x`.
- Stick to lowercase with underscores (`snake_case`).
- Avoid starting variable names with numbers or using reserved keywords.

Chapter Three

Control Flow and Loops

Control flow and loops are foundational concepts in Python, enabling developers to build dynamic, decision-driven programs. They allow code to respond to conditions and repeat tasks efficiently, eliminating redundancy. This chapter will break down these elements to ensure a deep understanding for beginners.

Decision-Making with If, Else, and Elif

In programming, decision-making enables software to react differently based on conditions. Python **if**, **else**, and **elif** statements are tools for this purpose.

Structure of If Statements

The **if** statement tests a condition and executes the block of code beneath it if the condition evaluates to `True`.

Example:

```python
age = 18
if age >= 18:
    print("You are eligible to vote.")
```

Else: Default Actions

The **else** block handles cases where the condition is `False`.

Example:

```python
age = 16
if age >= 18:
    print("You are eligible to vote.")
else:
    print("You are not eligible to vote.")
```

Elif: Multiple Conditions

Use **elif** to test multiple conditions in sequence.

```python
score = 85
if score >= 90:
    print("Grade: A")
elif score >= 80:
    print("Grade: B")
else:
    print("Grade: C or below")
```

Common Pitfalls

- Indentation Errors: Ensure proper indentation as Python uses it to define blocks.
- Logical Errors: Test complex conditions thoroughly.

For and While Loops Explained

Loops automate repetitive tasks, making programs concise and efficient.

For Loops: Iterating Through Collections
The **for** loop is used to iterate over sequences like lists, strings, or ranges.
Example:
```python
fruits = ["apple", "banana", "cherry"]
for fruit in fruits:
    print(fruit)
```

The Range Function

The `range()` function generates a sequence of numbers.
```python
for i in range(5):
    print(i)
```

While Loops: Conditional Repetition
While loops execute as long as a condition remains true.
Example:

```python
count = 0
while count < 5:
    print(count)
    count += 1
```

Key Differences Between For and While
- **For** loops are ideal when the number of iterations is known.
- **While** loops excel in situations where the condition's fulfillment is uncertain.

Working with Break, Continue, and Pass Statements

Python provides control statements to modify the normal flow of loops.

Break: Exiting Loops Early

The **break** statement terminates the loop when a condition is met.

```python
for num in range(10):
    if num == 5:
        break
    print(num)
```

Continue: Skipping Iterations

The **continue** statement skips the current iteration and proceeds to the next.

```python
for num in range(10):
    if num % 2 == 0:
        continue
    print(num)
```

Pass: Placeholder for Future Code

The **pass** statement does nothing; it's useful as a placeholder.

```python
for _ in range(3):
    pass  # Implementation pending
```

Best Practices for Using Control Statements

- Use break judiciously to avoid overly complex logic.
- Avoid overusing *continue*, as it can make loops harder to read.

Practical Examples and Exercises

1. Creating a Simple Voting Eligibility Checker

Prompt the user for their age and display eligibility based on input.

```python
age = int(input("Enter your age: "))
if age >= 18:
    print("You can vote.")
else:
    print("You cannot vote.")
```

2. Number Guessing Game

Use loops and conditions to implement a game where the user guesses a randomly generated number.

```python
import random
target = random.randint(1, 10)
while True:
    guess = int(input("Guess the number (1-10): "))
    if guess == target:
        print("Correct!")
        break
    else:
```

```python
    print("Try again.")
```

3. Filtering Even Numbers from a List*
Write a script that filters even numbers using loops and conditions.

```python
numbers = [1, 2, 3, 4, 5, 6]
even_ numbers = []
for num in numbers:
    if num % 2 == 0:
        even_ numbers.append(num)
print(even_ numbers)
```

4. Generating a Multiplication Table
Create a multiplication table using nested loops.

```python
for i in range(1, 11):
    for j in range(1, 11):
        print(f"{i} x {j} = {i*j}", end="\t")
    print()
```

Chapter Four

Functions and Modules

Understanding Functions and Their Uses

Functions are reusable blocks of code designed to perform specific tasks. They reduce repetition and improve code readability by enabling programmers to encapsulate logic into callable units. A function in Python starts with the `def` keyword, followed by a function name, parentheses for parameters, and a colon.

Why Functions Matter

-Code Reusability: Functions allow programmers to write a piece of logic once and use it in multiple places. This is critical in large projects where repetitive code increases maintenance costs.

-Readability: Code segmented into functions is easier to understand, debug, and modify.

- Scalability: Functions support modular programming, allowing you to tackle complex problems by dividing them into smaller, manageable pieces.

Example:

```python
def greet(name):
    return f"Hello, {name}!"


print(greet("Alice"))
```

This simple function, `greet`, demonstrates how functions encapsulate logic and provide flexibility.

Built-in vs. User-Defined Functions

Built-In Function: Python comes with functions like `len()`, `type()`, and `print()`. These cover general use cases.

- User-Defined Functions: When built-in options don't suffice, you can define custom functions tailored to your needs.

Common Mistake: Forgetting the return statement. A function without `return` implicitly returns `None`.

Writing Your Own Functions

Creating effective user-defined functions involves understanding parameters, scope, and return values.

Parameters and Arguments

Parameters are placeholders for input values in a function definition, while arguments are the actual values passed when calling a function. Python supports:

-Positional Arguments: Matched by position.

-Keyword Arguments: Matched by parameter name.

-Default Parameters: Provide default values if arguments are omitted.

- Variable-Length Arguments: Use `args` and `kwargs` for flexible inputs.

Example:
```python
def calculate_ area(length=1, width=1):
    return length * width

print(calculate_ area(5, 3)) # Positional
print(calculate_ area(width=4, length=2)) # Keyword
print(calculate_ area()) # Default
```

Scope and Lifetime

Variables in Python have a scope:

-Local Variables: Declared within a function and inaccessible outside.

-Global Variables: Declared outside any function and accessible everywhere.

-Nonlocal Variables: Used in nested functions to access enclosing scope variables.

Example:

```python
def outer_function():
    x = 10
    def inner_function():
        nonlocal x
        x += 1
    inner_function()
    return x
```

Best Practices

1. Keep functions short and focused on a single responsibility.
2. Use descriptive names to clarify purpose.
3. Include comments for complex logic.

Importing and Using Python Modules

Modules extend Python's capabilities by grouping related functions, variables, and classes.

Understanding Modules

-Built-In Modules: Part of Python's standard library (e.g., `math`, `os`).
-External Modules: Created by third parties and installed via `pip`.
-Custom Modules: Written by users for project-specific needs.
Example:

```python
import math
```

```
print(math.sqrt(16)) ```
```

Importing Techniques

1. Entire Module: `import module_name`
2. Specific Functionality: `from module_name import function_name`
3. Alias: `import module_name as alias`

Example:
```python
from math import sqrt as square_root
print(square_root(25)) ```
```

Creating Custom Modules

Custom modules are simple to create:
1. Save Python functions in a `.py` file (e.g., `utilities.py`).
2. Import them in other scripts.

Example:
```python
# utilities.py
def add(a, b):
    return a + b

# main.py
from utilities import add
print(add(3, 4))
```

Organizing Modules with Packages
Packages are directories containing a collection of modules. An `__init__.py` file in the directory marks it as a package.

Advanced Function and Module Usage

Exploring advanced techniques like lambda functions, decorators, and module optimization:

Lambda Functions

Lambda functions are concise anonymous functions defined using the `lambda` keyword.

Example:
```python
double = lambda x: x * 2
print(double(5))
```

Decorators

Decorators modify function behavior dynamically without altering the function code.

Example:
```python
def decorator_function(func):
  def wrapper():
    print("Before the function call.")
    func()
```

```
    print("After the function call.")
    return wrapper

@decorator_function
def say_hello():
    print("Hello!")

say_hello()```
```

Optimizing Module Imports
Importing selectively minimizes memory usage and improves performance. Avoid wildcard imports (`from module_name import`) in production code.

Chapter Five

Working with Data

Data is the foundation of programming, and Python provides versatile tools to handle, manipulate, and process data efficiently. In this chapter, we delve into Python's data structures and techniques to manage and work with information effectively. Whether it's storing simple lists, organizing complex datasets, or reading from and writing to files, this chapter equips you with the essential skills to handle data like a pro.

Lists, Tuples, and Dictionaries

Understanding Lists

Lists are one of Python's most versatile data structures, designed for storing ordered collections of items. They allow you to store items of various data types, such as integers, strings, or even other lists.

- Creating Lists

To create a list, use square brackets (`[]`) and separate items with commas.

```python
fruits = ["apple", "banana", "cherry"]
```

- Accessing and Modifying Items

Lists are zero-indexed, meaning the first item has an index of `0`. You can access or modify items using their indices.

```python
fruits[1] = "blueberry"   # Changes "banana" to "blueberry"
```

- Common List Operations

Python offers a wide range of list operations, such as appending items, removing elements, and slicing for subsets.

```python
```

```
fruits.append("orange")
fruits.remove("apple")
print(fruits[1:3])  # Outputs items at index 1
and 2 ```
```

Exploring Tuples

Tuples are immutable sequences, meaning their contents cannot be changed after creation. They are ideal for fixed collections of items.

- Creating Tuples

Use parentheses (`()`) to define a tuple.

```python
dimensions = (1920, 1080)
```

- Tuple Operations

While immutable, tuples support indexing and slicing, making them useful for storing constant datasets.

Dictionaries: Key-Value Pairs

Dictionaries store data as key-value pairs, offering efficient lookups and flexible data management.

- Creating Dictionaries

    Use curly braces (`{}`) and separate keys and values with colons (`:`).

```python
student = {"name": "John", "age": 25, "grade": "A"}
```

- Accessing and Updating Data

    Access values by their keys and update or add new pairs dynamically.

```python
student["age"] = 26
student["major"] = "Computer Science"
```

- Practical Use Cases

Dictionaries are invaluable for managing structured data, such as JSON objects or configurations.

Strings and String Manipulation

Basic String Operations

Strings in Python are sequences of characters, offering extensive functionality for manipulation.

-Creating Strings

Strings can be defined using single (`'`) or double (`"`) quotes.

```python
greeting = "Hello, World!"
```

- String Methods

Python's built-in string methods enable formatting, searching, and modifying strings.

```python
print(greeting.lower())    # Converts to lowercase
print(greeting.replace("World", "Python"))
```

String Formatting

Python supports modern and efficient string formatting using `f-strings` and the `.format()` method.

- Using F-Strings

```python
name = "Alice"
print(f"Welcome, {name}!")
```

- Using `.format()`

```python
print("Welcome, {}!".format(name))
```

Working with Multiline Strings

Multiline strings are enclosed in triple quotes (`"""` or `"""`). They are useful for documentation and preserving line breaks.

```python
message = """Dear User,
Thank you for choosing Python.
Best regards,
The Team"""
```

File Handling: Reading and Writing

Opening and Closing Files

Python's built-in `open()` function allows you to work with files in various modes:

- `r`: Read mode
- `w`: Write mode (overwrites)

- `a`: Append mode (adds content)

- Opening a File
```python
file = open("example.txt", "r")
content = file.read()
file.close()
```

- Using the `with` Statement
  The `with` statement ensures proper file closure and simplifies syntax.
```python
with open("example.txt", "r") as file:
    content = file.read()
```

Reading Files
- Read Entire Content
```python
content = file.read()
```

``

- Reading Line by Line
```python
for line in file:
    print(line.strip())
```

Writing to Files
Python makes it easy to write data to files, either by overwriting or appending.

- Writing Example
```python
with open("output.txt", "w") as file:
    file.write("Hello, Python!")
```

Practical Applications
File handling is essential for data logging, configuration management, and processing large datasets.

Chapter Six

Object-Oriented Programming

Object-Oriented Programming (OOP) is a cornerstone of modern software development, and Python, as a versatile programming language, fully supports OOP principles. This chapter will introduce you to the fundamentals of OOP, covering key concepts such as classes, objects, inheritance, and polymorphism. By the end of this chapter, you will be able to organize your code more effectively, re-use components efficiently, and design scalable applications.

The Basics of Classes and Objects

At its core, Object-Oriented Programming revolves around the concept of **object** and

classes. Understanding these concepts is the first step toward mastering OOP.

-What is a Class?
A class serves as a blueprint for creating objects. It defines the structure and behavior that the created objects will have. Think of a class as a recipe, and objects as the dishes prepared following that recipe. Classes encapsulate data for the object and methods that define what the object can do.

Example:
```python
class Dog:
    def __init__(self, name, age):
        self.name = name
        self.age = age

    def speak(self):
        return f"{self.name} says Woof!"
```

```
```

In the example above, `Dog` is a class that has an `__init__` method to initialize the object's attributes, `name` and `age`, and a method called `speak`, which defines the behavior of the dog (making it speak).

- What is an Object?
An object is an instance of a class. Once you define a class, you can create as many objects as you need from that class. These objects have the properties and behaviors described by the class.

Example:
```python
my_dog = Dog("Rex", 5)
print(my_dog.speak())    # Output: Rex says Woof!
```

In this case, `my_dog` is an instance (or object) of the `Dog` class, with the attributes `name` and `age` set to "Rex" and 5, respectively.

- The Importance of the `__init__` Method
The `__init__` method in Python is a special method, often called the constructor. It's automatically called when a new object of the class is instantiated. It allows you to initialize the object's attributes.

Creating Methods in Classes
Methods are functions defined inside a class and are used to describe the behaviors of the objects. You already saw a simple example of a method (`speak`) in the previous code. Here, we will explore more

complex methods and how they can manipulate object data.

Example:
```python
class Car:
    def __init__(self, make, model, year):
        self.make = make
        self.model = model
        self.year = year

    def display_info(self):
        return f"{self.year} {self.make} {self.model}"

    def start_engine(self):
        return f"The {self.model}'s engine is now running."
```

Accessing Object Properties and Methods

To interact with an object's properties or methods, you use the dot (`.`) operator. For example:

```python
my_car = Car("Toyota", "Camry", 2020)
print(my_car.display_info())    # Output: 2020 Toyota Camry
print(my_car.start_engine())  # Output: The Camry's engine is now running.
```

Inheritance: Reusing Code for New Classes

One of the key benefits of OOP is **inheritance**, where a new class can inherit the properties and methods of an existing class. This promotes code reuse, reduces redundancy, and makes it easier to maintain and extend code.

- Creating a Subclass

A subclass is a class that inherits from another class. The subclass can access all methods and properties of the parent class but can also add its own methods and properties, or even override the parent class methods.

Example:
```python
class ElectricCar(Car):
    def __init__(self, make, model, year, battery_size):
        super().__init__(make, model, year)
        self.battery_size = battery_size

    def display_battery_info(self):
        return f"This car has a {self.battery_size}-kWh battery."
```

- The `super()` Function

In the example above, the `super()` function is used to call the constructor of the parent class `Car` from the subclass `ElectricCar`. This ensures that the new class inherits the properties and methods of the parent class while allowing for additional functionality to be added.

Polymorphism: Same Interface, Different Behaviors

Polymorphism allows for different classes to be treated as instances of the same class through a shared interface. It enables the same method to behave differently depending on the object that calls it.

- Method Overriding
Polymorphism often involves overriding a method in a subclass. This means that a subclass can provide a specific implementation for a method that is already defined in the parent class.

Example:
```python
class Dog:
    def speak(self):
        return "Woof"

class Cat:
    def speak(self):
        return "Meow"

def animal_sound(animal):
    print(animal.speak())

my_dog = Dog()
```

```
my_cat = Cat()

animal_sound(my_dog)  # Output: Woof
animal_sound(my_cat)  # Output: Meow
```

In this example, even though both `Dog` and `Cat` have a `speak` method, each animal speaks differently. The `animal_sound` function can take any object that implements the `speak` method, demonstrating polymorphism.

Encapsulation: Protecting Data and Methods

Encapsulation is the practice of bundling the data (attributes) and the methods that operate on that data within a single unit or class. It also refers to restricting access to some of the object's components, which can prevent unintended interference and misuse of the data.

– Private and Public Attributes
In Python, you can denote an attribute as private by prefixing it with two underscores (`__`). This makes the attribute inaccessible from outside the class, helping to protect the integrity of the data.

Example:
```python
class BankAccount:
    def __init__(self, balance):
        self.__balance = balance  # Private attribute

    def deposit(self, amount):
        if amount > 0:
            self.__balance += amount
        else:
```

```
        print("Deposit amount must be
positive.")

    def get_balance(self):
        return self.__balance
```

- Accessing Private Attributes
Though private attributes are not directly accessible, you can provide getter methods (like `get_balance`) to allow controlled access to those attributes.

Example:
```python
account = BankAccount(1000)
print(account.get_balance())    # Output: 1000
account.deposit(200)
print(account.get_balance())    # Output: 1200
```

Abstract Classes and Methods

An **abstract class** is a class that cannot be instantiated on its own and serves as a blueprint for other classes. Abstract methods are methods that are declared in an abstract class but are meant to be implemented by subclasses.

– Creating Abstract Classes
In Python, you can create an abstract class using the `abc` module, which stands for **Abstract Base Class**. Abstract classes allow you to define methods that must be implemented in any subclass.

Example:
```python
from abc import ABC, abstractmethod

class Animal(ABC):
```

```python
    @abstractmethod
    def sound(self):
        pass

class Dog(Animal):
    def sound(self):
        return "Woof"
```

Here, the `Animal` class cannot be instantiated directly because it contains an abstract method. The `Dog` class must implement the `sound` method to be instantiated.

Mastering OOP in Python

Mastering Object-Oriented Programming in Python is crucial for writing clean, efficient, and maintainable code. By understanding the key concepts of classes, objects, inheritance, polymorphism, encapsulation, and abstract classes, you will be able to structure your Python programs with greater flexibility and scalability.

Chapter Seven

Error Handling and Debugging

Understanding Errors in Python

Errors in programming are inevitable, especially for beginners. In Python, errors are classified into two primary types: **syntax errors** and **runtime errors**.

- Syntax Errors: These occur when Python's parser encounters a line of code that violates its grammatical rules. For example, forgetting a colon at the end of an `if` statement or mismatched parentheses.

  - Example: `if x > 5 print(x)` *(missing colon)*
  - The Python interpreter will highlight syntax errors immediately.

- Runtime Errors: These occur during the execution of code, even when the syntax is correct. Examples include dividing by zero or attempting to access an invalid list index.

   - Example: `result = 10 / 0` *(division by zero)*

Understanding the root causes of errors is the first step toward effective debugging. Errors should be viewed not as failures but as opportunities to learn and refine your code.

Using Try-Except for Exception Handling

The `try-except` block is Python's primary mechanism for handling runtime errors gracefully. It prevents the program from crashing when encountering an error and allows you to define alternative actions.

- Basic Syntax:

```python
try:
    # Code that may raise an error
    result = 10 / x
except ZeroDivisionError:
    # Action to take if an error occurs
    print("You cannot divide by zero.")
```

- Multiple Exceptions: Handle multiple error types by specifying them individually or grouping them.

```python
try:
    result = 10 / int(input("Enter a number: "))
except (ValueError, ZeroDivisionError) as e:
    print(f"An error occurred: {e}")
```

- The Else Clause: Executes code only if no exception occurs.

```python
try:
    result = 10 / 2
except ZeroDivisionError:
    print("Division by zero!")
else:
    print("Division successful!")
```

-Finally Block: Always executes, regardless of exceptions.

```python
try:
    file = open("data.txt", "r")
except FileNotFoundError:
    print("File not found.")
finally:
    print("Closing operation.")
```

Debugging Tips for Beginners

Debugging is a critical skill that helps identify and fix errors efficiently. Below are proven strategies to enhance debugging:

1. Print Statements: Use print statements to inspect variables and control flow.

```python
x = 5
print(f"x before operation: {x}")
x = x + 10
print(f"x after operation: {x}")
```

2.Use Debugging Tools: IDEs like PyCharm, VS Code, or Jupyter Notebook offer built-in debuggers for setting breakpoints, stepping through code, and examining variables.

3. Review the Traceback: Python's error messages include a traceback that specifies the error type, message, and the line number where it occurred. Analyzing this can often point directly to the problem.

4. Isolate the Problem: Simplify your code by testing small sections to pinpoint where the error arises.

5. Rubber Duck Debugging: Explain your code line-by-line to a friend, colleague, or even an inanimate object like a rubber duck. This process often reveals overlooked issues.

6. Consult Documentation and Forums: Python's official documentation and community forums like StackOverflow are invaluable resources for understanding errors and seeking solutions.

By mastering error handling and debugging, Python programmers can write robust, efficient, and error-resistant code, even as beginners.

Chapter Eight

Practical Python Applications

Automating Everyday Tasks

Python is a powerful tool for automating repetitive and mundane tasks, saving time and reducing errors. Whether you are organizing files, sending emails, or extracting data from spreadsheets, Python provides libraries and functions to make automation accessible even for beginners.

File Organization and Management
Using Python's `os` and `shutil` libraries, you can create scripts to rename, move, or delete files in bulk. For instance, a Python script can automatically sort files into folders based on their extensions, helping you maintain a clutter-free desktop.

```python
import os
import shutil

# Example: Organize files by extension
def organize_files(directory):
    for file in os.listdir(directory):
        file_path = os.path.join(directory, file)
        if os.path.isfile(file_path):
            ext = file.split('.')[-1]
            folder_path = os.path.join(directory, ext)
            os.makedirs(folder_path, exist_ok=True)
            shutil.move(file_path, folder_path)

organize_files('/path/to/directory')
```

Automating Emails

With the `smtplib` library, Python enables email automation. This is particularly useful for businesses to send out newsletters, reminders, or notifications. Combined with libraries like `email.mime`, you can format your emails to include text, HTML, or attachments.

Data Extraction and Manipulation
Python simplifies working with data through libraries like `pandas` and `openpyxl`. These tools allow you to read, write, and process data in spreadsheets or databases, enabling you to automate reports or process bulk datasets.

Data Analysis with Python

Python is renowned for its robust data analysis capabilities. It has become the go-to language for data scientists and analysts due to its simplicity and the power of its libraries.

Getting Started with Pandas

The `pandas` library is the cornerstone of data analysis in Python. It provides data structures like DataFrames, which make handling tabular data intuitive. Here's an example of how you can use `pandas` to analyze sales data:

```python
import pandas as pd

# Load data
data = pd.read_csv('sales_data.csv')

# Analyze data
print(data.describe())
```

```
print(data.groupby('Category')['Revenue'].
sum())
```

Data Visualization with Matplotlib and Seaborn
Visualization is critical for understanding data. Python's `matplotlib` and `seaborn` libraries offer powerful tools for creating insightful plots, from simple line charts to complex heatmaps.

Using NumPy for Numerical Computation
The `numpy` library complements data analysis by providing efficient operations for numerical data. It is particularly useful for matrix operations and statistical calculations.

Building a Simple Web Scraper

Web scraping allows you to extract data from websites for analysis or personal use. Python's `requests` and `BeautifulSoup` libraries make it easy to fetch and parse web content.

Understanding the Basics
A web scraper mimics a browser to request web pages and then extracts the needed data. Always ensure your scraping adheres to a website's terms of service.

Building a Scraper with BeautifulSoup
Here's an example of a script that extracts product names and prices from an e-commerce site:

```python
import requests
from bs4 import BeautifulSoup

# Request webpage
response = requests.get('https://example.com/products')
soup = BeautifulSoup(response.text, 'html.parser')

# Parse data
for product in soup.find_all('div', class_='product-item'):
    name = product.find('h2').text
    price = product.find('span', class_='price').text
    print(f"{name}: {price}")
```

Using Scraped Data

Once data is scraped, you can save it to a file or database for further processing. For instance, price comparison tools use scraping to gather competitive pricing data.

Each subchapter here delves into practical applications, explaining both the "why" and the "how" in an engaging and informative manner. These sections highlight Python's versatility, demonstrating how it empowers users to solve real-world problems efficiently.

Chapter Nine

Working with Libraries

Python libraries are a cornerstone of its power and versatility, enabling programmers to achieve complex tasks with minimal effort. This chapter explores key libraries essential for beginners and their practical applications. Understanding these libraries will elevate your Python skills and prepare you for more advanced projects.

Popular Python Libraries for Beginners

Overview of Libraries

A Python library is a collection of pre-written code that allows you to perform various tasks without writing every line of code from scratch. Libraries save time, improve efficiency, and enhance productivity. While Python boasts thousands of libraries, some are particularly beneficial for beginners.

Key Libraries to Learn

1. NumPy (Numerical Python)

- Purpose: Efficient numerical computation.

- Uses: Working with arrays, performing mathematical operations, and processing large datasets.

- Example: Computing the mean or standard deviation of an array in seconds.

2. Pandas

- Purpose: Data manipulation and analysis.

- Uses: Organizing data into tabular formats, cleaning datasets, and performing operations like grouping and merging.

- Example: Loading CSV files into a DataFrame for data analysis.

3. Matplotlib
  - Purpose: Data visualization.
- Uses: Creating line graphs, bar charts, and scatter plots.
  - Example: Plotting sales data over months for a presentation.

4. Requests
  - Purpose: Sending HTTP requests.
  - Uses: Fetching data from web APIs.
- Example: Retrieving live weather data from an online API.

5. Beautiful Soup
  - Purpose: Web scraping.
- Uses: Extracting data from HTML and XML files.

- Example: Scraping prices of products from e-commerce sites.

Best Practicesto ensure compatibility.

Using Matplotlib for Basic Visualizations

- Install only what you need to keep your project lightweight.
- Read the documentation to understand library functionalities thoroughly.
- Use version control

Why Visualization Matters

Data is more impactful when represented visually. Python's Matplotlib library makes it easy to create clear, professional graphs to communicate findings effectively.

Getting Started with Matplotlib

- Installation: `pip install matplotlib`
- Basic Syntax: Import the library using `import matplotlib.pyplot as plt`.

Creating Basic Charts

1. Line Charts

    Ideal for showing trends over time.

    Example: Plot monthly sales data using:

    ```python
    plt.plot([1, 2, 3], [4, 5, 6])
    plt.title('Monthly Sales')
    plt.show()
    ```

2. Bar Charts

    Effective for comparisons across categories.

    Example: Compare revenue across regions.

3. Scatter Plots

    Useful for observing relationships between two variables.

Example: Plot customer age versus purchase amount.

Customization
- Add titles, labels, and legends for clarity.
- Adjust colors, line styles, and marker types for aesthetics.

Introduction to Pandas for Data Handling

What are Pandas?
Pandas transforms raw data into structured and analyzable formats. It simplifies handling CSVs, Excel sheets, and databases.

Key Features
-DataFrames: Two-dimensional data structures similar to Excel sheets.
- Series: One-dimensional arrays, often used for a single column of data.

Basic Operations

1. Loading Data

Load data from CSV files using:

```python
import pandas as pd
df = pd.read_csv('data.csv')
```

2. Data Cleaning

Handle missing values, duplicate entries, and inconsistent formatting.

Example:

```python
df.fillna(0, inplace=True)
```

3. Data Analysis

Perform operations like filtering, grouping, and aggregating.

Example: Calculate the average sales:

```python
```

```
avg_ sales = df['Sales'].mean()
```
```

```

Practical Applications
- Automating data reports.
- Cleaning messy datasets.
- Integrating with visualization libraries for dashboards.

Each section in this chapter equips you with the tools to harness Python libraries effectively, enabling you to solve real-world problems. The techniques and examples ensure you are ready to handle larger projects and dive deeper into specialized Python fields.

Chapter Ten

Advanced Beginner Topics

10.1 Working with APIs

Introduction to APIs

APIs (Application Programming Interfaces) are crucial for enabling communication between different software applications. As a beginner advancing in Python, understanding how to use APIs is essential for automating workflows, retrieving data from web services, and building integrations. APIs simplify complex programming tasks by providing a set of predefined operations, enabling developers to focus on implementing specific functionalities rather than reinventing the wheel.

How APIs Work

APIs act as intermediaries between two applications. For instance, when you use a weather app, it requests real-time weather data from an external API. This API fetches the information and delivers it to your application in a structured format like JSON or XML. Python, with its robust libraries, simplifies the process of working with APIs, allowing you to interact with web services efficiently.

HTTP Methods and Status Codes

To work with APIs effectively, it is crucial to understand HTTP methods:
- **GET:** Used to retrieve data from a server.
- **POST:** Sends new data to a server.
- **PUT:** Updates existing data.
- **DELETE**: Removes data.

Additionally, HTTP status codes provide feedback about the success or failure of an API request:
- 200: Success.
- 404: Resource not found.
- 500: Server error.

Using Python Libraries for APIs

Python's `requests` library is a popular choice for interacting with APIs. It offers an intuitive way to make HTTP requests. For example:

```python
import requests

response = requests.get('https://api.example.com/data')
if response.status_code == 200:
    print(response.json())
```

Practical API Integration Example

Suppose you want to build a script that fetches current exchange rates. Using the `requests` library:

```python
import requests

url = 'https://api.exchangerate-api.com/v4/latest/USD'
response = requests.get(url)

if response.status_code == 200:
    data = response.json()
    print(f"1 USD equals {data['rates']['EUR']} EUR")
else:
    print("Failed to fetch exchange rates.")
```

This example demonstrates retrieving and parsing data from a public API. You can extend this functionality by integrating it into applications, such as currency converters.

Best Practices for Using APIs

-Understand API Documentation: Familiarize yourself with the API's endpoints and authentication requirements.

-Handle Errors Gracefully: Include logic to handle timeouts, failed requests, and unexpected responses.

-Secure API Keys: Never hard code API keys in your scripts. Use environment variables or secure vaults.

10.2 Understanding Python Decorators

What Are Decorators?

Decorators in Python are a powerful tool for modifying or enhancing the behavior of functions or methods. They are commonly used to manage repetitive tasks, such as logging, access control, or performance monitoring, without altering the original function's logic.

How Decorators Work

A decorator is a function that takes another function as input, adds some functionality, and returns a new function. The syntax for applying a decorator is straightforward:

```python
def
decorator_function(original_function):
    def wrapper_function():
```

```
    print("Wrapper executed before the
function.")
    return original_function()
  return wrapper_function


@decorator_function
def display():
  print("Display function ran.")
```

Practical Applications of Decorators

1.Logging: Automatically log the execution of functions for debugging or monitoring.

2.Authentication: Ensure only authorized users access certain functions.

3.Caching: Store results of expensive computations to avoid redundant calculations.

Creating Custom Decorators

Suppose you want a decorator to measure execution time:

```python
import time

def timing_decorator(func):
    def wrapper(*args, **kwargs):
        start_time = time.time()
        result = func(*args, **kwargs)
        end_time = time.time()
        print(f"{func.__name__} executed in {end_time - start_time} seconds.")
        return result
    return wrapper

@timing_decorator
def sample_function():
    time.sleep(2)
    print("Function executed.")
```

sample_function()
```
```

This decorator records and prints the execution time of `sample_function`, demonstrating how decorators simplify reusable functionality.

Writing Tests with Python

Importance of Testing
Testing is integral to software development, ensuring code reliability and minimizing bugs. In Python, writing tests allows you to verify that individual components of your program behave as expected. As a beginner, mastering testing early can save you significant debugging time in larger projects.

Types of Tests

1. Unit Tests: Validate individual units of code, such as functions.

2. Integration Tests: Test the interaction between multiple components.

3. End-to-End Tests: Simulate real-world scenarios to ensure the application works as intended.

Using Python's `unittest` Module

Python's built-in `unittest` module provides a structured way to write and execute tests. Here's an example:

```python
import unittest

def add(a, b):
    return a + b

class
TestMathOperations(unittest.TestCase):
```

```python
def test_ add(self):
    self.assertEqual(add(2, 3), 5)
    self.assertEqual(add(-1, 1), 0)

if __ name__ == '__ main__':
    unittest.main()
```

This script tests the `add` function and ensures it produces the expected results.

Test-Driven Development (TDD)

TDD emphasizes writing tests before implementing code. This approach ensures the code meets the predefined requirements and reduces errors.

Best Practices for Writing Tests

- Write tests for edge cases to handle unexpected inputs.
- Use descriptive names for test cases for better readability.

- Organize tests into logical groups for easier maintenance.

These advanced topics help you move beyond the basics and prepare you for tackling more complex Python projects. They provide a foundation for exploring fields like data science, web development, and automation with confidence.

Chapter Eleven

Final Projects

Building a To-Do List Application

The practical application of Python begins with solving real-world problems. A to-do list application is one of the simplest yet most useful tools you can create. In this subchapter, we will walk through the steps to design and build a functional to-do list application that allows users to add, delete, and view tasks.

Introduction to the Project

A to-do list application is a perfect beginner's project because it incorporates various programming concepts. This project uses lists, functions, and user input while giving you a taste of file handling if you decide to save tasks for later use.

Step 1: Structuring the Program

Before diving into the code, it is essential to outline the program's flow. A well-structured program has:

1.An Interactive Menu: Options for adding, viewing, and deleting tasks.

2. A Data Storage System: In-memory lists for simplicity or file storage for persistence.

3. Error Handling: Preventing crashes from invalid inputs or unexpected scenarios.

Step 2: Creating the Interactive Menu

The interactive menu is the program's user interface. Using Python's `while` loop, you can keep the program running until the user decides to exit. For example:

```python
def display_ menu():
    print("\nTo-Do List Application")
    print("1. Add a Task")
```

```python
    print("2. View Tasks")
    print("3. Remove a Task")
    print("4. Exit")

def main():
    tasks = []
    while True:
        display_menu()
        choice = input("Enter your choice: ")
        if choice == '1':
            add_task(tasks)
        elif choice == '2':
            view_tasks(tasks)
        elif choice == '3':
            remove_task(tasks)
        elif choice == '4':
            print("Goodbye!")
            break
        else:
            print("Invalid choice. Please try again.")
```

The menu acts as the entry point, directing the user to different functionalities.

Step 3: Adding Tasks

The `add_task` function allows users to input a task, which is then appended to the list.

```python
def add_ task(tasks):
    task = input("Enter the task: ")
    tasks.append(task)
    print(f"Task '{task}' added successfully!")
```

Tips for Improvement:

- Use unique IDs for each task for better management.
- Include a priority level to sort tasks.

Step 4: Viewing Tasks

Displaying tasks in a readable format ensures that users can easily track their progress.

```python
def view_ tasks(tasks):
    if not tasks:
        print("Your to-do list is empty.")
    else:
        print("\nYour To-Do List:")
        for i, task in enumerate(tasks, start=1):
            print(f"{i}. {task}")
```

Enhancements:

- Add completion status (e.g., pending or done).
- Sort tasks by priority or due date.

Step 5: Removing Tasks

The `remove_task` function lets users delete tasks by specifying the task number.

```python
def remove_task(tasks):
    if not tasks:
        print("Your to-do list is empty.")
    else:
        view_tasks(tasks)
        try:
            task_num = int(input("Enter the task number to remove: "))
            removed_task = tasks.pop(task_num - 1)
            print(f"Task '{removed_task}' removed successfully!")
        except (ValueError, IndexError):
            print("Invalid task number. Please try again.")
```

Challenges Addressed:

- Handling invalid inputs gracefully.
- Ensuring the program doesn't crash if the list is empty.

Step 6: Adding File Storage

For enhanced functionality, integrate file handling to save and retrieve tasks.

```python
def                    save_ tasks(tasks,
filename="tasks.txt"):
    with open(filename, 'w') as file:
        for task in tasks:
            file.write(task + "\n")
    print("Tasks saved successfully!")

def load_ tasks(filename="tasks.txt"):
    try:
        with open(filename, 'r') as file:
```

```
    return [line.strip() for line in file]
except FileNotFoundError:
    return []
```

Saving tasks ensures that they persist even after the program is closed, providing a real-world application experience.

Step 7: Enhancing User Experience

To make the application user-friendly, consider the following:

1. User Feedback: Provide clear messages for each action.

2. Customization: Allow users to change the interface (e.g., themes or colors).

3. Error Prevention: Use input validation to guide users.

Building a to-do list application is an excellent exercise for beginners. It not only reinforces basic concepts like loops and lists but also introduces more advanced ideas such as file handling. By completing this project, you gain confidence in your ability to solve problems using Python.

Creating a Basic Calculator

A calculator is one of the most fundamental tools for solving mathematical problems. Writing a Python program to create a basic calculator helps beginners practice core concepts such as functions, conditionals, loops, and user input handling. This subchapter explains how to build a robust calculator that performs basic arithmetic operations like addition, subtraction, multiplication, and division.

Introduction to the Calculator Project

The calculator project involves creating a program that allows users to input two numbers and select an operation. While the goal is simple, the implementation provides a solid foundation for understanding Python programming. It's also a stepping stone for more advanced projects, such as scientific or graphical calculators.

Step 1: Planning the Program Structure

Before writing code, outline the program's flow:
1. Display Menu: Show available operations (e.g., addition, subtraction).
2.Get Input: Prompt the user to enter numbers and choose an operation.
3.Perform Calculation: Execute the selected operation.

4. Display Results: Show the output of the calculation.

5.Repeat: Allow the user to perform multiple calculations until they choose to exit.

Step 2: Designing the User Interface

A clear and user-friendly interface is crucial. Use Python's `print` function to display the menu and guide users:

```python
def display_menu():
    print("\nBasic Calculator")
    print("Select an operation:")
    print("1. Addition (+)")
    print("2. Subtraction (-)")
    print("3. Multiplication (*)")
    print("4. Division (/)")
    print("5. Exit")
```

The menu provides users with an intuitive way to interact with the program.

Step 3: Getting User Input

Use the `input()` function to get numbers and the desired operation from the user. Validate the inputs to avoid runtime errors.

```python
def get_numbers():
    while True:
        try:
            num1 = float(input("Enter the first number: "))
            num2 = float(input("Enter the second number: "))
            return num1, num2
        except ValueError:
            print("Invalid input. Please enter numeric values.")
```

Key Considerations:
- Ensure users input valid numbers.
- Handle cases where the input is not a number gracefully.

Step 4: Implementing Operations
Each arithmetic operation can be defined as a separate function. This modular approach makes the code clean and reusable.

```python
def add(a, b):
    return a + b

def subtract(a, b):
    return a - b

def multiply(a, b):
    return a * b
```

```python
def divide(a, b):
    if b != 0:
        return a / b
    else:
        return "Error: Division by zero is not allowed."
```

Best Practices:
- Keep operations simple and focused.
- Return meaningful error messages for invalid operations, like division by zero.

Step 5: Main Program Logic

Integrate the menu, user input, and operations into a loop. This ensures the program runs until the user decides to exit.

```python
def main():
```

```python
while True:
    display_menu()
        choice = input("Enter your choice (1-5): ")
    if choice == '5':
            print("Exiting the calculator. Goodbye!")
        break
    elif choice in ('1', '2', '3', '4'):
        num1, num2 = get_numbers()
        if choice == '1':
            print(f"The result is: {add(num1, num2)}")
        elif choice == '2':
                print(f"The result is: {subtract(num1, num2)}")
        elif choice == '3':
                print(f"The result is: {multiply(num1, num2)}")
        elif choice == '4':
```

```
        print(f"The result is:
{divide(num1, num2)}")
    else:
        print("Invalid choice. Please try
again.")
```

Enhancements:
- Allow users to input multiple operations at once (e.g., a chain calculation like `2 + 3 * 4`).
- Add functionality for advanced operations such as exponentiation or modulus.

Step 6: Error Handling and Validation
Anticipate common errors, such as:
1. Invalid Menu Selection: Ensure the user can only select valid options.
2. Division by Zero: Prompt the user to enter a non-zero denominator.

3.Non-Numeric Inputs: Provide clear instructions when the user enters invalid data.

By implementing robust error handling, you create a user-friendly experience that prevents crashes.

Step 7: Expanding Functionality

To take this project further, consider adding:
Advanced Operations: Include functions like square root, power, and logarithms.
Memory Feature: Store the last calculation result for reuse.
Graphical Interface: Use libraries like Tkinter to build a visual interface.

For example, a power function can be added easily:

```python
def power(a, b):
    return a ** b
```

A basic calculator is a straightforward yet effective project for consolidating foundational Python skills. By building this program, you learn how to handle user input, structure programs, and implement error-handling techniques. Moreover, the project can evolve with your skills, making it a valuable tool throughout your learning journey.

Making Your Own Command-Line Tool

Command-line tools are versatile, lightweight applications used for automation, data manipulation, and system management. This project introduces you to the creation of a Python-based command-line tool (CLI), providing valuable insight into how Python integrates with the command line to solve practical problems.

Introduction to Command-Line Tools
Command-line tools are designed to perform specific tasks efficiently without requiring graphical user interfaces. They are commonly used by developers, system administrators, and data analysts. With Python's robust libraries like `argparse`, `sys`, and `os`, creating a custom command-line tool becomes straightforward.

Why Build a CLI Tool?
- Simplify repetitive tasks, such as renaming files or processing data.

- Learn how Python interacts with the operating system.
- Create reusable tools for personal or professional use.

In this subchapter, we will build a CLI tool for organizing files in a directory by grouping them into subfolders based on file type.

Step 1: Planning the Tool

Before coding, define the tool's purpose and structure:

1. Purpose: To organize files in a directory by file type (e.g., documents, images, videos).

2. Features:

   - Scan a directory and identify file types.

   - Create subfolders for each file type (e.g., `.jpg` files go into an "Images" folder).

- Move files into their corresponding subfolders.

3. Command-Line Interface:
  - Accept a directory path as input.
  - Display the organization progress.

Step 2: Setting Up the Project

To start, create a new Python file, such as `file_organizer.py`. Import essential libraries:

```python
import os
import shutil
import argparse
```

- `os`: Interacts with the file system.
- `shutil`: Moves files and creates directories.

-argparse`: Handles command-line arguments.

Step 3: Using Command-Line Arguments
With `argparse`, you can make your tool accept user input directly from the terminal. This is how you define and parse arguments:

```python
def parse_ arguments():
                    parser    =
argparse.ArgumentParser(description="Or
ganize files in a directory by file type.")
        parser.add_ argument("directory",
type=str, help="Path to the directory to
organize")
    return parser.parse_ args()
```

-Description: Explains the tool's functionality.
- Positional Argument: Requires the user to input the directory path.

The command to run this tool will look like:
```bash
python file_organizer.py /path/to/directory
```

Step 4: Scanning the Directory

Scan the specified directory to identify files and their types:

```python
def get_files_by_type(directory):
    file_types = {}
    for root, _ , files in os.walk(directory):
        for file in files:
            file_extension = file.split('.')[-1].lower()
            if file_extension not in file_types:
```

```python
file_types[file_extension] = []

file_types[file_extension].append(os.path.j
oin(root, file))
    return file_types
```

Explanation:
- `os.walk`: Iterates through the directory
and its subdirectories.
- File Grouping: Files are grouped by
extension (e.g., `.jpg`, `.pdf`).

Step 5: Creating Subfolders
After identifying file types, create
subfolders for each type.

```python
def     create_folders_by_type(directory,
file_types):
    for file_type in file_types:
```

```python
        folder_path = os.path.join(directory,
file_type.capitalize() + "s")
                        os.makedirs(folder_path,
exist_ok=True)
    return True
```

Key Points:
- **Dynamic Folder Creation**: Subfolders are created based on file types.
- **Error Prevention**: Use `exist_ok=True` to avoid errors if the folder already exists.

Step 6: Moving Files into Subfolders

Move files from their current location to the appropriate subfolders.

```python
def move_files(file_types, directory):
```

```python
for file_type, files in file_types.items():
    for file in files:
        destination = os.path.join(directory,
file_type.capitalize()      +      "s",
os.path.basename(file))
        shutil.move(file, destination)
```

-`shutil.move`: Relocates files from source to destination.
- Dynamic Paths: File destinations are determined based on their type.

Step 7: Main Function
Combine all components into a cohesive program.

```python
def main():
    args = parse_arguments()
    directory = args.directory
```

```
if not os.path.isdir(directory):
    print("Invalid directory path. Please
try again.")
    return

print(f"Organizing files in: {directory}")
            file_types        =
get_files_by_type(directory)
    create_folders_by_type(directory,
file_types)
    move_files(file_types, directory)
    print("File organization complete!")
```

Program Flow:

1. Parse the directory path.

2. Validate the path to ensure it exists.

3. Organize files using the defined functions.

Step 8: Error Handling

Anticipate and handle common errors:
1. Invalid Directory: Notify the user if the directory doesn't exist.
2. Permission Errors: Provide feedback if the program cannot create folders or move files.

Example:
```python
try:
    os.makedirs(folder_path, exist_ok=True)
except PermissionError:
        print(f"Permission denied: Unable to create folder {folder_path}")
```

Step 9: Testing the Tool

Thoroughly test your CLI tool with various scenarios:

1. Directories with mixed file types.
2. Empty directories.
3. Large directories with thousands of files.

Step 10: Adding Extra Features

To enhance the tool, consider the following:

1. Exclude Certain Files: Add an option to exclude specific file types.
2. Log File: Save a log of all moved files for reference.
3. Dry Run: Display what the program will do without making changes.

Example for a dry run:

```python
def dry_run(file_types, directory):
    for file_type, files in file_types.items():
```

```
    print(f"Files of type '{file_type}' will be
moved                              to
'{directory}/{file_type.capitalize()}s'.")
```

Building a command-line tool solidifies your understanding of Python and introduces practical skills for interacting with the operating system. This project not only highlights Python's versatility but also demonstrates the value of automating repetitive tasks. With your CLI tool, you've taken another significant step toward mastering Python.

Conclusion

Charting Your Python Journey

1. Continuing Your Python Journey

Learning Python doesn't stop with this book—it's a stepping stone into a world of limitless possibilities. With the foundational skills you've gained, you are now equipped to explore advanced topics such as data science, artificial intelligence, web development, and beyond.

Your next step depends on your goals. If you're drawn to data, delve into libraries like Pandas and NumPy to manipulate datasets or Matplotlib to visualize data trends. For those interested in web development, frameworks such as Django and Flask provide tools to create dynamic and scalable websites. Python is also widely used in automation, enabling you to streamline repetitive tasks at work or home.

Practice is the cornerstone of mastering any skill. Challenge yourself by building projects that align with your interests. Start small—a personal budget tracker, a simple chatbot, or even a text-based game. Over time, work your way up to more complex applications like a weather app using APIs or a data analysis dashboard. Projects not only solidify your knowledge but also help you showcase your skills to potential employers or collaborators.

Engage with the Python community, which is one of the most welcoming and resource-rich programming communities in the world. Platforms like Stack Overflow, GitHub, and Python.org host discussions, open-source projects, and mentorship opportunities. Attending meetups, hackathons, and conferences also opens doors to networking and professional growth.

2. Resources for Advanced Learning

The world of Python programming is dynamic and ever-evolving. To stay ahead, invest time in reliable resources. Online courses, such as those on platforms like Coursera, edX, or specialized training hubs, offer advanced tutorials and certifications. Books like **Automate the Boring Stuff with Python** and **Fluent Python** (after exhausting your beginner's level knowledge) provide deep dives into niche topics.

Reading Python's official documentation, though intimidating at first, is an invaluable habit to cultivate. It allows you to understand Python's core features directly from its maintainers. Furthermore, follow blogs and newsletters like Python Weekly to stay updated on the latest developments.

Experimentation is another form of learning. When you encounter a new concept or feature, try implementing it in a sandbox project. For instance, when learning about Python's multiprocessing capabilities, create a program that processes multiple tasks simultaneously, such as sorting large datasets or running parallel downloads.

For those pursuing specific career paths, targeted certifications can be a game-changer. Certifications such as Microsoft's Python Programming certification or Google's IT Automation with Python Professional Certificate validate your skills and boost your professional profile.

3. Staying Updated with Python Trends

Technology evolves rapidly, and Python is no exception. Staying updated with the latest trends and best practices ensures your skills remain relevant. In recent years, Python has expanded its influence in areas like artificial intelligence (AI) and machine learning (ML). Libraries such as TensorFlow, PyTorch, and scikit-learn make Python indispensable in these fields.

Cybersecurity is another emerging domain where Python plays a critical role. Tools like Scapy, Nmap, and Python's extensive cryptography libraries empower professionals to create secure systems and analyze potential threats.

In web development, microservices architecture is gaining traction, and Python frameworks like FastAPI are being widely adopted. Learn to create APIs that are efficient, scalable, and adhere to modern standards.

Another burgeoning area is quantum computing. While still in its infancy, Python libraries such as Qiskit offer access to this revolutionary technology, providing opportunities to learn and experiment in groundbreaking computational fields.

Beyond tools and libraries, focus on writing efficient and maintainable code. Adopting best practices such as adhering to PEP 8 guidelines, employing test-driven development (TDD), and utilizing version control systems like Git ensures that your projects are professional and collaborative-ready.

Lastly, contribute to the Python ecosystem by creating your own libraries or contributing to existing open-source projects. It's a rewarding way to give back to the community while showcasing your expertise.

With the knowledge you've gained and the opportunities ahead, Python can become both a tool and a creative outlet. This journey is yours to shape—start building, experimenting, and growing. Python is more than a language; it's a gateway to innovation. Let this book be the first chapter in your story of programming success.

Appendices

Appendix A: Python Keywords and Built-In Functions

Python keywords and built-in functions form the backbone of programming in Python. Mastering these fundamental elements empowers you to write clear, concise, and effective code. In this section, we will comprehensively break down Python's keywords and its built-in functions, ensuring you're equipped to use them with confidence.

1. Python Keywords

Python keywords are reserved words that convey specific instructions to the Python interpreter. They cannot be used as identifiers, such as variable names or function names. Python 3.10 introduced several new keywords, and it is crucial to familiarize yourself with the latest additions to stay updated.

Here's a categorized breakdown:

- Control Flow:
  Keywords like `if`, `elif`, `else`, `for`, `while`, and `break` dictate the flow of your program. They ensure the program executes specific code blocks based on defined conditions.

- Boolean and Null Values:
  The keywords `True`, `False`, and `None` represent boolean values and the absence of a value. Knowing their behavior is essential for writing logical conditions and handling null cases.

- Function and Class Definitions:

Keywords like `def`, `return`, `class`, and `yield` help in defining reusable functions and creating custom classes. These structures are vital for scaling your projects efficiently.

- Data Manipulation:

`in`, `not in`, `is`, and `is not` are keywords that allow you to evaluate membership and identity of objects. They are frequently used in loops and conditionals.

- Error Handling:

`try`, `except`, `finally`, `raise`, and `assert` enable robust error handling. Understanding how to use them can prevent your programs from crashing unexpectedly.

- Advanced Use Cases:

Keywords like `global`, `nonlocal`, `lambda`, and `async` are designed for specific use cases. For example, `async` allows for asynchronous programming, while `lambda` enables creating anonymous functions.

2. Built-In Functions

Python offers a vast library of built-in functions designed to simplify tasks. These functions can be categorized as follows:

- Data Type Conversion:

Functions such as `int()`, `float()`, `str()`, `list()`, and `dict()` are invaluable for converting data types. For instance, converting a string to an integer ensures numeric operations can be performed seamlessly.

- Mathematical Operations:

`abs()`, `round()`, `min()`, `max()`, and `sum()` are essential for performing mathematical computations without the need for importing additional libraries.

- Input and Output:

The `print()` function is used for output, while `input()` accepts user input. Knowing how to format output using `print()` makes your programs more user-friendly.

- Iterables and Sequences:

Functions like `range()`, `len()`, `enumerate()`, and `zip()` allow efficient handling of sequences. They are especially useful in loops and data processing tasks.

- File Handling:

Built-in functions such as `open()`, `read()`, `write()`, and `close()` are critical for working with files. These functions enable reading from and writing to files directly within your Python scripts.

- Miscellaneous Functions:
   Python's `help()` and `dir()` functions are indispensable tools for developers. While `help()` provides documentation about Python modules or functions, `dir()` lists all attributes of an object, helping you understand its structure.

Practical Tips for Keywords and Functions
1. Practice Regularly:
   Write small code snippets that use keywords and functions in different scenarios. Experimentation leads to better understanding.
2. Avoid Overcomplication:

Use built-in functions wherever possible instead of reinventing the wheel. Python's simplicity lies in its ability to minimize code complexity.

3. Stay Updated:
Python evolves rapidly. Familiarize yourself with changes in each version to maximize your proficiency.

Appendix B: Quick Reference: Python Syntax

A quick reference for Python syntax ensures you don't lose time searching for solutions to common coding challenges. Let's distill Python's syntax into clear, actionable points.

1. Indentation Rules
Python's use of indentation in place of brackets is a hallmark of its syntax. Each

block of code must be consistently indented, typically by four spaces. Errors in indentation result in a `IndentationError`.

Example:
```python
if True:
    print("This is correctly indented")
else:
    print("Fix the indentation")
```

2. Naming Conventions
Python encourages readable code with guidelines for naming variables, classes, and functions.

- Variables: Use `snake_case` for variable names. Example: `user_name = "John Doe"`
- Classes: Use `PascalCase`. Example: `class UserProfile:`

- Constants: Use all uppercase letters. Example: `PI = 3.14`

3. Comments and Docstrings

Use `#` for single-line comments and triple quotes (`"""`) for multi-line docstrings.

Appendix C: Glossary of Terms

This glossary provides concise definitions of essential Python concepts and terminology.

- Argument: A value passed to a function when it is called.
- Decorator: A function that modifies the behavior of another function or method.
- Generator: A function that returns an iterator and allows lazy evaluation.
- PEP 8: Python's official style guide.

These appendices provide a robust reference, equipping beginners with the tools they need to build strong Python programming foundations. Let me know if you'd like further customization!

www.ingramcontent.com/pod-product-compliance
Lightning Source LLC
LaVergne TN
LVHW051342050326
832903LV00031B/3700

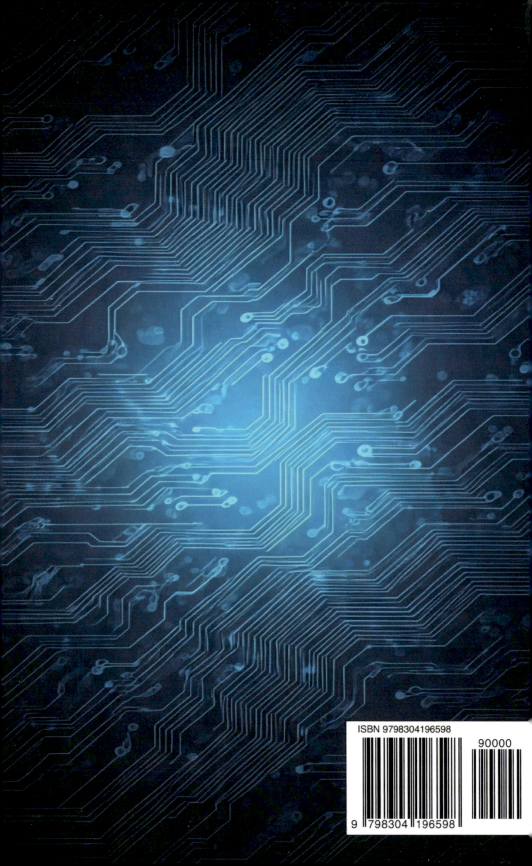

ISBN 9798304196598